THE POWER OF
COLOR

**Harness the creative and healing
energy of color**

THE POWER OF
COLOR

**Harness the creative and healing
energy of color**

C Y N T H I A   B L A N C H E

L ANSDOWNE

CONTENTS

C O N T E N T S

INTRODUCTION

Color is a living energy. It is everywhere there is light. Animals, birds and insects use color to propagate the species and for protection. Flowers use color to attract the insects that will cause pollination. Every person on the planet emits colors that are perceived by all others, no matter how unconsciously, and those colors inform us about each other. Color has played an integral part in religion throughout the world, throughout time, and it has always been used in its many and varied forms to uplift people's spirits and bring them joy.

The purpose of this book is to help you understand what color is, the power it has in the natural world, and the power it can have for you. It will show you how to recognize your colors; it will demonstrate how color can affect you both positively and adversely; and then suggest ways in which you can use color to increase calm, energy and richness in your life. You can also use color to help heal physical and emotional problems, in conjunction with your medical practitioner's treatment.

Often, when people see an abstract painting by a famous artist, their response is: "A child could do that!" This is not far from the truth, and therein lies the painter's secret.

What children can see, adults generally no longer can. Colors are vivid and exciting to children. They don't care if the tree in front of them has brown bark and green leaves: sometimes they like to make the trunk blue and the foliage red. Then perhaps their parents tell them that the tree has a brown trunk and green leaves and make them change their painting. Children often like to color outside the lines, then adults try to make them color inside the lines. Why should a child do this? Because that is how it is in the adult world. There are rules to follow if you are going to get on in life, and coloring outside the lines breaks the rules. So the child struggles to paint inside the lines and make their trees true to life — and imaginations are restrained and tamed; perceptions dim, and colors lose their intensity.

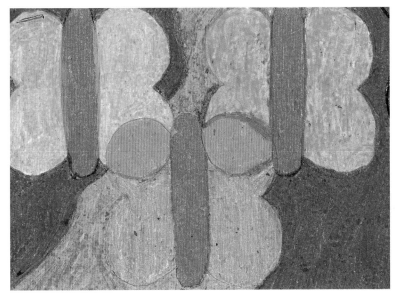

Zoe Abbott, age 12

This book will show you how you can unleash your creativity. Indulge yourself in finger painting, using whatever colors you like, no matter what the subject. Make colorful soft toys for the children in your life or for those with nothing who would value them. Dismiss the rules of planting by color and create an original and exciting garden that will never bore you.

Most of the time we have little consciousness of color, unless it is a factor in choosing a new car, a piece of clothing, or something to decorate our homes. How often do we notice the colors of the flowers in the park as we sit on the grass eating our lunch? Noticing a sunset, a sunrise or a rainbow thrills us, yet how often do we break our daily routine to watch a sunset or look at a rainbow? A few minutes a day watching the sun go down in the west or rise from the eastern horizon can give us a deep sense of peace in much the same way as does meditation.

Even if you are the most restrained of adults and consider yourself unimaginative or uncreative, by focusing on the power of color, you can open the doors of perception to recapture your innate creativity and to see how color can help heal you. In the process, you will transform your life by learning to see through the eyes of the child you once were.

THE POWER OF COLOR

Color — Perceptions of a Living Energy

When light reflects off the surface of an object we perceive color. Light consists of different wavelengths in the visible spectrum as well as ultraviolet light which is invisible to our eyes. These are all part of the electromagnetic spectrum. Radiation within the wavelengths of the visible spectrum gives color its intensity and therefore its energy. The longest wavelength, the one with the lowest frequency, is red. The shortest wavelength, the one with the highest frequency, is violet.

Things appear to be of a particular color because substances within them absorb certain wavelengths and reflect others. The chlorophyll within grass absorbs the wavelengths of all colors in the visible spectrum but one. This wavelength is reflected from the grass and we perceive it as the color green.

The intensity of color we see depends on the light-absorption factors of the object's surface. A black surface absorbs all colors, so reflects nothing back. A white surface, on the other hand, reflects all wavelengths. And when all the colors in light combine they become white.

Wavelengths contain radiation. Radiation is energy. Energy is living.

Pigments

Substances that absorb color are known as pigments. The color of your skin comes from the pigment melanin; the green in plants is chlorophyll; and the pigments that cause bright colors in plants are carotenoids (yellow, orange, and red), quinones (yellow, orange, red, purple or green), and flavonoids (yellow, bluish reds). Plant pigments are absorbed by animals and humans when they eat the plants.

Many societies throughout history have believed that color holds great power for promoting that which is good and protecting the individual from all that is evil. People have always used color to adorn themselves for both sacred and secular purposes, and to decorate their environment. Traditionally, they used pigments that came from rocks, plants and anything else that would produce a colored powder or liquid. Nowadays color is used for a multitude of purposes, and the majority of pigments are artificially created, though many of the finest quality artists' pigments are still derived from traditional sources.

The Prism

A prism is a transparent piece of glass, usually with triangular ends, that has been cut to precise angles and planes. When you look through a prism, you see the rainbow array of white light broken into its component wavelengths or colors. Every edge you look at through a prism is accompanied by a bright aura of color. The common names for these colors are red, orange, yellow, green, blue, indigo and violet.

Looking through a prism is a remarkable experience. Triangular prisms can be obtained quite easily. One such source could be your local optometrist.

How Color Affects Our Moods, Emotions, and Sense of Well-Being

While some people are more sensitive to color than others, we all react to it in some way. For instance, when you walk into a room, you may not notice any particular color, but you will feel either uplifted or depressed or somewhere in between — you may feel suddenly energized or flat. Every color with the exception of black puts out energy, so it is only logical that they affect us, but everyone reacts differently to color and its combinations. Cool colors, such as blues, cool greens and grays, generally reduce the intensity of a person's vibrations. This may be a great thing if you are strung out, anxious or just wish to feel calm and serene; but if you have a low-key personality, these colors could rob you of vitality.

The fashion industry understands how color affects people's moods, as do the home decorating, advertising and marketing industries. Color is integral in forming our perceptions of the world, in every area of our lives, both secular and religious. It is indeed a powerful influence.

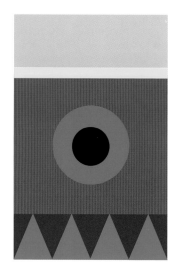
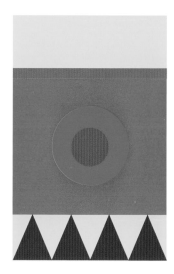

Color Sayings

We often refer to colors when describing our reaction to people or situations. "She's green with envy"; "He's got the blues today"; "I see red whenever I think about that incident!"; "You look a little off-color today."

This is because we associate certain moods with particular colors. These may differ according to historical and cultural contexts, but how did they begin? It could be that we respond subliminally to the personal rainbow that surrounds all living things — the aura. Colors emit vibrations. So do we.

Auras are discussed in HEALING WITH COLOR on page 50.

Color and Culture

Just as individuals react in a variety of ways to color, so do entire cultures. Cultural associations with color depend on what aspects of the personality are considered strong or weak, fortunate or unfortunate, happy or sad. Black is the color for funerals in the West, while Chinese cultures use white. Western and Japanese brides wear white; most other Asian cultures dress the bridal couple in red.

Cultural perceptions of color also vary. Green and blue might be given the same name in some cultures, which is not surprising when you consider that some Westerners can't tell the difference between bluish green and greenish blue, both of which they might refer to as "blue" or "green".

All cultures recognize black and white, but the Eskimos have 17 words for white. The next most commonly recognized color is red, followed by yellow or green, and then yellow and green. Blue is the next color most recognized, followed by brown. Colors such as pink, purple, orange and gray are sometimes not recognized.

Color in Our Everyday Lives

Color plays a role in every aspect of our lives. Designers of hospitals, offices and other places of business are now conscious of the effect color has on people and decorate accordingly. The natural world is full of color, from bugs to birds and weeds to trees. People are also full of color — in their skin, hair, eyes, as well as in their personalities. We all radiate color. Whether or not you believe in the concept of the aura, humans certainly radiate energy, and energy radiates color.

Color surrounds us when we walk down the street or drive past billboards; when we sit in a chair watching television; in our places of work. It is in every shop window, every vacant lot, and a multitude of colors can be found in even the smallest pebble. Color is everywhere, but how much of it are we conscious of seeing? The more color you notice around you, the richer your day will be. Discovering color where you least expect to find it — for it is there — can be an exciting experience.

We are most conscious of color in our clothing, our homes and our cars. But we are often unaware of how adding or removing even a tiny amount of color can alter the mood of a room or outfit. Despite our lack of consciousness of the color that surrounds us, we love it. And when a color doesn't please us, we tend to reject it forcefully.

Every color has a positive and negative effect, depending on whose home it is decorating or who is wearing it. So when we choose colors for our clothing or for decorating, we go straight to those colors that reinforce the way we feel.

When you understand the relationship between certain colors and how they affect you, you will understand a great deal about your personality and how you see yourself. The way we dress tells everyone how we expect to be seen, and this is not always the same as how we wish to be seen — but that can be changed.

Color Can Give You Power

Everybody has a favorite color or colors. We like to wear clothing of that color, and use it when we decorate our homes. This color makes us feel better.

But color can do much more than simply please us. Have you ever noticed that on some days you just can't tolerate the idea of wearing, say, the red pullover, and choose the gray one instead? Color can give you the power to control the way people respond to you. For instance, if you are going for a job promotion or new job, you should choose colors that make you feel confident, but which are not threatening to your proposed employers. Red would be threatening to a conservative employer, while cleverly worn, it would be just right for vital, progressive industries.

Think about color when it is important that you create a particular impression. But remember that the colors you wear have to be your colors, otherwise they will not work for you.

COLOR IN THE NATURAL WORLD

Rainbows, Sunsets, Seas and Skies

From the beginning of human history much romance and drama has been attached to rainbows, sunsets, seas and skies. Gods, magic, love, blessings, anger and revenge have been attributed to these extraordinary, yet everyday, miracles of light.

The varying shades of blue that you see when you look at the sky are created by reflections of light from the sun as it passes through Earth's atmosphere. The color of the sky differs dramatically depending on where you are on the globe, on the season, the time of day, and on the weather. The color of clouds is determined by a combination of the sun's light, the amount of water they are carrying and how high they are. Rainbows appear when the sun's light hits each drop of water in rain, spray or fog. Seas reflect the sky and their intensity of color depends on the depth of the water, the color of the sky, and their levels of pollution.

Polluted water and atmospheres reflect a muddy, cloudy appearance. You will find when you read page 50 in HEALING WITH COLOR, how psychological pollution or physical illness can make your aura just as murky.

The Harmony of Colors in Nature

In nature all colors harmonize, sometimes dramatically, at other times with serenity. There is no such thing as a clash of color in nature; however, when putting together colors that have been artificially created, you would do well to avoid putting colors together that will clash, create disharmony or bring out anger or depression.

While someone may hate green in his or her home or clothing, he or she usually still loves the green of grass and foliage. And people who dislike blue, will still love a blue sky or sea.

Color and the Kingdom of Animalia

There are two kingdoms of living things on this planet — Animalia and Plantae. Here we are concerned with the organisms in the kingdom of Animalia and how they use color to protect themselves and attract mates, both of which are essential for the survival of the species.

Coloration involves pigments known as biochromes (biological tissues that reflect or transmit light) and the form or structure of the organism. As well as serving to attract mates and emit warnings, coloration also contributes to balancing the organism's body temperature by absorbing or reflecting light (energy) from the sun. The lighter the organism's color, the more energy it will reflect, and the cooler the organism will be; the darker an organism's color, the more energy it will absorb, and the warmer it will be.

Mimicry is when a species disguises itself as something else to protect itself from predators. An organism often uses color to resemble an object in its environment or a creature that frightens the predator. For instance, many non-poisonous insects resemble in color and form insects that are poisonous and so are less likely to be eaten. Insects that are poisonous to predators are often colored black and yellow or black with red spots or stripes. Many non-poisonous species have mimicked this warning coloration for their protection.

An extraordinary example of mimicry is found in some organisms, including certain species of fish, moths and caterpillars. When the hawk moth is disturbed or threatened, it rhythmically opens and closes its wings, revealing markings resembling large eyes, detailed in color and form, that bear a striking similarity to the eyes of birds or mammals. The *Leucorhampha* caterpillar is just an ordinary caterpillar until it raises its thorax, which is now expanded, waving from side to side and striking at its predator. The predator is seeing a "snake's head"

16

depicted in the finest detail, including all the scales and two shining eyes. Another curious example of mimicry is when an insect seems to have two heads, one at each end. The most colorful butterfly species which have this characteristic are found in South America.

The most common form of **camouflage** is the use of color to disguise the organism or to help it blend into its surroundings. Organisms from the smallest through to the largest are colored to make it seem invisible to its predators or its prey. Human beings took this lesson from the animals and use camouflage in military operations.

Advertisement is the term used to refer to coloring that makes the organism highly visible, either for attracting a mate for reproduction or for warning predators. A good example of sexual advertising is displayed by the East African baboon, the mandrill. The male has cheeks of bright blue, a red nose, a yellow beard, and buttocks of purple and pink — no doubt highly attractive to the less colorful female.

We are all familiar with birds and their often brightly colored plumage. Their colors and patterns serve as protective coloration or for sexual display. In the animal kingdom the male usually has the adornment, while the females are relatively dull in appearance. However, the females have all the power — she gets to choose her mate from the many who compete for her favors.

Rapid color change is coloration displayed by certain sea animals, amphibians and reptiles when excited. Waves of spectacular color will ripple across the bodies of octopus and some mollusks. Most fish, reptiles and amphibians take several minutes up to several hours to complete a color change. Rapid color change is the result of migrating pigments in specialized cells known as chromatophores.

Flash color is a phenomenon that occurs when an organism displays a striking color in movement, but is inconspicuous at rest. Flash color is displayed in many sea and land organisms. A demonstration can be observed in grasshoppers. When resting on the ground, the grasshopper blends in with its background. Once threatened, it leaps up and its predator will see a brilliant flash of red, blue or yellow.

Can Animals See Color

Until scientists can look through the eyes of an animal, they can only speculate as to what colors animals can see. However, there appears to be a correlation between the colors on an animal's body and the colors it can see. Mammals, other than humans and apes, have not demonstrated that they can see color. Birds have a good color vision, and those that pollinate, such as the hummingbird, are mainly attracted to bright red flowers. Evidence that birds can see most colors is displayed during their mating rituals and their reactions to the warning colors of insects. Fish can see at least the colors with which they want to blend, especially those species that change color to match their environment, and perhaps also identify potential mates through color recognition.

Insects seem to have a strong color sense though, in the case of bees and other pollinating insects, their perception of color differs from ours in that they are also sensitive to ultraviolet light. Houseflies see blue and dislike it. Mosquitoes are especially attracted to black but can also see yellow and white. In an experiment conducted in Oregon some years ago, seven men wore shirts of different colors. In only 30 seconds, the black shirt had attracted 1,499 insects while the white shirt attracted only 520.

The Color Spectrum as seen by color-seeing animals

ANIMAL	Red	Orange	Yellow	Green	Blue	Indigo	Violet
Primates	✓	✓	✓	✓	✓	✓	✓
Birds	✓	✓	✓	✓	✓	✓	
Fish and Lizards	✓	✓	✓	✓			
Bees	*Ultra-violet*	✓	✓	*Yellow green & blue green*	✓	✓	
Some Insects and Butterflies	✓ *(some species only)*	✓	✓	✓	✓	✓	✓

Why Flowers Are Colored

Flowers and insects have evolved together and are mutually dependent — flowers need insects to distribute pollen and insects need nectar for food. Color and scent are the most important means flowers use to attract birds and insects to their nectar and their pollen.

Bees, the most important pollinators among insects, are attracted to brightly colored flowers that are open during daylight hours. Bees do not see the color red as we see it; instead, they perceive ultraviolet light. The colors bees can see are yellow, orange, yellowish green, bluish green, blue, purple and violet. Bees follow both color and ultraviolet patterns on the flowers. Flowers pollinated by bees are often purple, blue or yellow, or exhibit patterns in these colors. These patterns that are so pleasing to our sense of beauty are landing sites and "follow these lines to the nectar" guides for pollinators.

Wasp-attracting flowers are generally brownish purple in color.

Butterflies have a similar sense of color to bees, although some butterfly species can see the color red. Flowers that are commonly pollinated by butterflies are intensely colored, are often red, and provide landing sites on open, flat petals. Moths are night creatures and are attracted to light-colored or white flowers that are open at night.

In the tropics and southern temperate zones, birds are probably as important as insects in pollinating flowers. Birds have powerful vision, and a strong color sense that resembles our own. They see the red to green part of the visible spectrum most clearly, and flowers pollinated by birds are generally red. Birds are also attracted to patterns comprised of complementary colors, such as orange and blue or green and red.

The Importance of Color in Human History

Color has always been significant to humans. No doubt our first use of color pigments was in sacred rituals, in camouflage, and to imbue warriors with power in battle. In many societies, color is used to distinguish one social class from another.

Societies that use color used for ritualistic purposes ascribe very particular meanings to each color they use, and these will differ from society to society. But whatever their meanings, color represents power — power to attract gods; power to ensure fertility; power to hunt; protection against the elements; and power to repel demons, ghosts or enemies.

In many societies, throughout history, color has been thought to encourage the process of linking people to the universe and to nature.

Some Comparative Meanings of Colors in Traditional Societies

Red is the sacred color of war for many North American tribes. In Papua New Guinea, the color red symbolizes prosperity. Red is associated with blood in Africa and is the color of life and death. In India, red serves spiritual and social purposes — it is the main color for marriage, and for the ascetic is one of the colors of fire. In the Japanese religion Shinto, red is the symbol of the rising sun and the color of life itself. For the Chinese, red is the color of heroes and generals, and is the color worn by the bride at her wedding.

Blue is frequently used to depict gods for it has both spiritual and erotic associations. A blue face in China, however, symbolizes cruelty. In the Japanese kabuki theater, blue outlines on a painted face indicate a bad character, while in different combinations, blue can represent nature gods and the spirits of ancestors.

White is worn by the relatives for funerals in traditional Chinese cultures and for weddings in the West. In various parts of the world it symbolizes the supernatural world. For promoting magic and meditation in India, people focus on a white-colored Vishnu. In Chinese theater, a white face represents brutality and depravity, while a small amount of white on the face indicates the lowliest of people. A white-painted face in traditional Japanese society separates the nobility from the sun-darkened lower classes.

Bright yellow is the imperial color of China, but in its duller tones yellow represents reticence. In Chinese theater, the white-painted faces of actors portraying heavenly beings are outlined in imperial yellow.

Black outlining around the eye protects some groups from the Evil Eye. When Vishnu is portrayed as the destroyer of enemies, he is colored black; however, in the Indian kathakali dance theater, those characters regarded as repellent are painted black. Strong black outlines on the white-painted face in Chinese theater show an impetuous character. In ancient Egypt, black represented order and fertility. In Japan and the West, black is the color of mourning, although in Japan, the deceased is dressed in white.

Green is often the color of tranquillity and life. The gentle Egyptian god Osiris is green-skinned; while in some Indian paintings, Vishnu will be portrayed as greenish blue, showing him as the god of water, air, and space. But green can also represent devils and demons in the Chinese theater.

Traditional Sources of Natural Pigments

Red — blood, carmine from the cochineal insect, cinnabar, flower pigments, henna, lead, madder, red sandalwood paste, red ochre, safflower.

Blue — ground powders from azurite, cobalt, indigo, lapis lazuli, turquoise, flower pigments.

Black — charcoal, galena, lampblack, manganese, soot.

White — ash, chalk, clay, gypsum, kaolin, lime, white lead, marble dust, rice powder.

Yellow — orpiment, plant saps, sandalwood bark, sulfur, turmeric, yellow chromium, yellow ochre.

Green — chrome green oxide, malachite powder, plant saps.

General sources — colored feathers from birds, shells, plant dyes, flower petals, seeds, ground gem stones.

How Some Tribal Societies Use Color

South America

Body painting is of the utmost importance for the jungle peoples of South America. Complexity of pattern and refinement of color and line make each person a work of art. While pattern and color represent specific functions shared by the group, individuals also have the freedom to express their own personal creativity.

Central America

The clothing worn by the people of the ancient Aztec, Mayan and Inca civilizations was vividly colored and decorated. Jewelry and exotic bird plumage were used for headdress decoration and woven into cotton fabric for cloaks. Pre-Columbian Americans painted and tattooed their skins, but decoration was not the major reason. The symbols and colors represented mystical, religious and social concepts, and were designed to link the human world with that of the spirits.

Africa

The peoples of Africa have a highly sophisticated sense of color. Their textiles and beadwork are masterpieces, as is the body art many tribal groups display. While beauty is a major consideration of body art, patterns and symbols reveal an individual's social rank, his or her history, group and religious beliefs. Particular patterns and colors link the person to the spirit world.

Color symbolism in Africa, like in so many other parts of the world, depends on occasion and varies from tribe to tribe and group to group. In the same way that the Eskimos have 17 words for white, each color in a given African language might have several words, depending on its intensity, its pattern, or the surface on which it appears.

In Africa white is usually linked to the world of spirits in one way or another, depending on where, when and why it is applied. It is sometimes used as a link to the spirit world, where it can represent spirits that induce terror or spirits that are there to help. White can also symbolize purity. Gentleness is often

Men from the Karo tribe in Ethiopia. Painting bodies with ochre and chalk releases the spirit; ostrich feathers show bravery.

(Inset photo on left hand page) This Songhai bride from Mali wears an elaborate headdress of gold filigree, silver coins, amber and glass beads.

represented by white while red can mean aggression. Red, often associated with human blood, can symbolize the life-force and the joy and good health this brings, but for other tribes it can represent the transience of life, therefore death and grief.

North America

Body painting was widespread among Native Americans, but the prairie tribes regarded it as of the greatest importance, relating it to their culture's existence and fate. Bodypainting displayed a warrior's achievements in battle and in the hunt — a lack of facial decoration reflected cowardice.

The many Native American tribes did not necessarily share the same color symbolism. Red, black and white, as well as feathers, were used a great deal. Red was generally regarded as a sacred color of war, denoting success and victory. For the Cherokees, white symbolized peace and happiness, and black represented death. For other tribes, white was the color of death and mourning and black the color of happiness.

Native Americans believed that this world and the next were interconnected. Every natural object was a means through which humans could communicate with the spirit world. To this end, along with song and dance, they decorated themselves with animal parts, feathers, beads and painting for good "medicine".

Color in the Ancient World

Egypt

Color was used widely in ancient Egypt. Columns, walls and floors were decorated with scenes from life and from myth, using splendid reds, ochres, greens, blues, whites and blacks. People's clothing began simply, but was adorned with color from semiprecious stones and collars of embroidered and beaded materials. As time went on, clothing became more decorative. Makeup was widely used by both sexes and men would henna their beards which they would then plait with gold threads. Beautiful blue or green faience (a glazed composition of ground quartz on earthenware) was used to make beads, jewelry, amulets and divine figurines. Faience, gold and other metals were used to make containers, plates and ornamental pieces.

Bronze Age Civilizations of the Aegean

This was the age of Homer's epic poems, *The Iliad* and *The Odyssey*; the age of Troy, Mycenae and Knossos and "wine-red" seas. Splendidly colored wall-paintings (frescoes) display the entertainment these societies enjoyed — dancing, boxing, athletics and the famous bull-leaping games. Clothing was elaborately colored and jewels highly prized. The Minoans were great artists; they observed nature closely and often used delicate lines and hues contrasted with splashes of stronger color.

Classical Greek

The Greeks created outstanding pottery, ceramics, jewelry and frescoes. Red and black were the preferred colors of pottery makers. Jewelry was quite rare in Classical Greece, but it began a magnificent era during the Hellenistic period. Delicate enamel work and polished stones increased the use of color in jewelry, as did glass which could be produced in any color. Mosaic, the art of decorating walls and floors with small colored components such as stone, minerals, tile, shell or colored glass, was extremely popular throughout the ancient world, and the amount of color used was limited only by the resources available to the owner of the building concerned. Greek mosaic contained representational motifs and pictures similar to wall-paintings and their pottery paintings.

The Romans

The Romans made distinctions in style between wall-paintings and floor decoration. Mosaic became simplified and made more use of materials of striking color, and varied from simple patterns to scenes containing people, animals, plants, birds, fish and mythological creatures. Frescoes of extraordinary beauty decorated the homes of the wealthy, the best examples being in Pompeii. The Romans loved ornamentation, both on themselves and in their homes.

The ancient Roman House of Neptune and Amphitrite in Herculaneum is named after this beautiful mosaic.

25

Color in the East

The East is synonymous with color. The people of Asia use color lavishly in adornment, decoration and religion. In Eastern societies, color is believed to protect individuals from ghosts and spirits, from the Evil Eye, and to promote health, wealth and happiness. Traditionally, color in clothing denoted a person's social class and religion.

There is a tradition of face painting in China and Japan. In early times it was believed to endow the person with magical powers. Later it came to represent an ideal of beauty, which is still evident in the makeup used by geishas. The characters in Chinese and Japanese traditional theater still paint their faces with the symbolic colors and patterns that denote heroes and villains, gods and demons, kings and the lowly.

Adornment

Though traditional costumes vary from country to country, opulence is common to all. Rich silks and brocades are embroidered with the images of mythological beings, spirits and ghosts, animal motifs, flowers and plants, using fine threads of pure gold, silver and colored silk. Jewelry in the form of collars, bracelets, necklaces and strings of beads interspersed with plaques and ornaments enhanced the whole figure. Decorations of jade, ivory, gold, silver, pearls, and precious and semi-precious stones were also used. These and the extraordinary headdress once worn by women in the East can still be seen in Chinese and Japanese theater and in museums.

Decoration

Wall-painting was an ancient art in China, India and Tibet. They display scenes in vivid color from each region's mythology, as well as gods, mythical beings, and symbols representing the universe. Dragons, horses, snakes, dogs and chariots were also popular motifs in wall-paintings, and appear widely on furniture, pottery, jewelry, scrolls and screens. Red and black seem to be the most potent colors in the East other than imperial yellow in the Chinese-based cultures. Faience and lacquerwork in glorious colors have from ancient times also been found throughout the East on jewelry, containers, furniture and ornaments.

In some places, highly colored mosaic floors have survived from very early times. Marble, colored stones, minerals, glass, tiles and shells were usually the materials used to create designs containing motifs with religious or mythical symbolism, or scenes from life and myth.

Carpet-making as we know it began in Persia, but many of the symbols famous in Persian carpets originated centuries earlier in China. The best Oriental carpets are made from silk or fine wool, and their designs can resemble brilliant jewels.

Religion

Certain colors in Asian religions represent specific aspects of good and evil. Color is also used to distinguish between the ranks of the priestly classes. Priests of the Japanese religion Shinto wear skirts in white, light blue or purple, a white kimono symbolizing purity, and a large-sleeved outer robe of various colors. In India, a Hindu teacher wears a yellow robe, while Indian Buddhist monks avoid primary colors, opting for mixed colors such as orange and brown. Tibetan Buddhist monks wear wine-colored robes.

Vast, vividly colored murals of complex spiritual motifs adorn the rooms of the Potala, the Dalai Lama's palace in Lhasa, Tibet. Some of the marvelous jewel-encrusted, gold representations of the Buddha and other spiritual artifacts can still be seen there, plus containers and furniture that are decorated in bright colors.

Artist's impression of a geisha by the author

Color and the West

With the exception of religion, the state and localized belief systems, such as religious and military cults, color has been regarded as largely decorative in the West. Even when a person's use of color was restricted because of his or her social status, it had more to do with the color's lavishness than its symbolism. Early European tribal groups, such as the Celts, believed color to be imbued with certain powers, and these beliefs would have continued through the ages wherever traditional practices of shamanism survived.

Color was central to the practices of alchemy in the Middle Ages, the basic colors being green, black, white, red and gold. The elements were considered to have colors: earth, black; water, white; fire, red; and air, yellow. These colors corresponded to the four humors that determined a person's health and well-being: black bile (melancholy); white phlegm (phlegmatic personality); red blood (heart and sanguine); and yellow bile (bad temper). The planets also had colors: yellow or gold for the sun; white or silver for the moon; red for Mars; purple for Mercury; blue for Jupiter; green for Venus; and black for Saturn.

Following the repressive arm of the Church during the Dark Ages and medieval period when rich colors and fabrics were permitted for the use of the aristocracy alone, the Renaissance brought color back into the world with all its vitality. Inspired by classical art, great works in grand style were created. Idealized figures and detailed landscapes of exquisite color by artists such as Titian, Michaelangelo, Botticelli, Raffaello dominated the walls and ceilings of palaces and cathedrals.

In later periods of art, color and subject matter became more subdued, until the end of the nineteenth century when the study of light and color was the main focus of the Impressionists. With the twentieth century, a revolt against realism began and color exploded onto the modern world, to stimulate ideas and question old attitudes and beliefs.

Modern psychotherapists know that colors have definite symbolism for people, though the symbolism is an individual one, and the practice of color therapy for both mental and physical ailments is growing. As we head toward the millenium, young people are dying their hair in multi-colors and painting their faces and bodies in colors and patterns. They seem to be forming tribe-like groups, identifying their own or others by specific colors and designs.

A Tree of Jesse, *stained glass window from 15th-century Germany.*

Religion

Color has always played an important symbolic role in religion in the West, just as it has in religion everywhere else in the world. In the Middle Ages, Biblical scenes were depicted in stained glass, richly colored icons, wall-paintings and illuminated manuscripts. Colors used have very specific meanings which date back to the days of the early Church. They continue to be used during specific festivals and feast days.

Colors That Unite and Inspire — Flags and Banners

National flags tap into a part of our consciousness that is both personal and collective and which causes us to react with unity in times of war or celebration. They are symbols that create feelings so profound that they can rarely be translated into words.

Flags as insignia of leadership and identification of friend or enemy probably originated in China or India. The royal flag carried all the attributes of the king and was the first object of attack. Its fall meant confusion or defeat.

Recognition of friend or foe is essential in war. In medieval Europe, when the identities of knights and soldiers were hidden behind their armor and friend sometimes killed friend, it became necessary to develop a system of identification. Thus heraldic arms were born, and by the twelfth century were well-established. In 1128 the Knights Templar adopted the Benedictine rule of life and the order's white wool habit which they marked with a red cross. This cross also appeared on their half-white, half-black banner.

Through the centuries, cities, states and nations have adopted colors and insignia which they then display on flags, standards and banners. Colors found in flags and banners are rarely if ever chosen merely for their beauty — even when representing a football club. The colors of a national flag symbolize the ideals that nation holds dear and the flag serves to remind the nation's citizens of those ideals.

The French national flag, the tricolor, consists of three vertical bands of equal width, displaying the national colors of France: blue, white and red. Though there is a long history of these three colors in France, it was not until the French Revolution in 1789 that the colors were combined to form the official flag of the country. Red and blue were the colors of Paris, while white was that of the

Bourbons, Louis XVI's family. The colors represented the joining of king and people in the Revolution. Citizens used the tricolor in their clothing, to decorate their furnishings, and by 1790, during the more radical phase of the Revolution, it was illegal to wear any other combination of colors.

Red is the color of socialism and red and yellow are traditional colors of China. The Chinese flag is red with a yellow five-pointed star (symbolizing the Communist Party's program) and four smaller yellow stars that represent the peasantry, the workers, the bourgeoisie and those capitalists who supported the revolution.

The Irish flag is green, white and orange. The green is for Catholics, the orange for Protestants (the original supporters of William of Orange), and the white symbolizes the desire that "beneath [the flag's] folds, the hands of the Irish Protestant and the Irish Catholic may be clasped in heroic brotherhood."

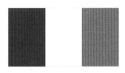

The flag colors of some Arab states are limited to red, white, green and black, which originally derive from the Caliphates of the early Islamic period.

The white background of the Korean flag expresses purity. The yin-yang symbol in the center represents the Buddhist concept of the fusion of opposites, and the trigrams at each corner represent three sequences. Working clockwise from upper left these are: summer, autumn, winter, spring; south, west, north, east; heaven, moon, earth, sun.

The United Kingdom's flag is made up from the cross of St. George (England), the cross of St. Andrew (Scotland) and the St. Patrick's cross of the Geraldine family of Ireland.

The flag of the United States of America, the Stars and Stripes, has a field of alternating stripes of red and white that represent the original 13 states, and a blue canton containing 50 stars which represent the 50 states of the Union.

Almost all clubs have "colors". During football season, their supporters display streamers from fences and windows, wear their team's colors, and use these colors to paint and decorate themselves from head to toe — sometimes very creatively. This way, people recognize each other's loyalties from their colors and band together to create powerful support for the club. The disadvantage is that fierce interactions, sometimes resembling minor wars, can occur between people wearing the colors of opposing teams.

Becoming Sensitive to Color

Take a moment to imagine that color has suddenly been taken from the world. There is no cosmic cinematographer to design gorgeous lighting like that of many black and white films — sharp black shadows contrasting with brightly lit areas, objects and people. Instead you are surrounded by tones of gray. Everywhere you look is gray, mostly in the mid-tonal range, variation upon variation of gray. How do you feel? Gray?

Now, dismiss all that gray from your mind and look around you. Look at what you are wearing. Look outside. How do you feel when you take in all the colors around you? Are they more vivid than they were before you did this little experiment? Now you know how important color is in our day-to-day lives.

Without color we'd feel flat and uninspired. Our music would be without color — that means it would have little tonal variation. And since we know that our moods and emotions are influenced by color, we would probably also have personalities with little or no color.

Most people who are color-blind do see color. They might have difficulties distinguishing certain colors, and one color, such as red or green, might seem gray, but it is very rare for a person to be only able to perceive shades of gray. However, people who are going blind might reach a stage where what little they can still see is gray.

A Little Exercise

Go into a vacant lot. Perhaps a building has been pulled down and there is nothing there but rubble. What are your first impressions? Do you find the scene ugly or boring? If so, take note of this. If not, make a note of how the scene strikes you. Now, pick a point, any point, and kneel on the ground. Study an area of ground about 12 inches (30 cm) square. What do you see? Sand, dirt, pebbles, rocks, blades of grass, bits of broken glass? Look at each item separately and notice the patterns and the colors radiating out from it. When you have finished, look at the square of ground as a whole. What do you see now?

Every natural thing, no matter how commonplace, is full of color and interesting patterns. You will find that if you do this often enough you will see color with greater intensity and in places you never expected to find it.

Street scene of the town of La Boca in Buenos Aires, Argentina.

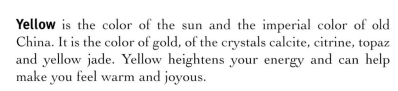

Some Colors and Their Effects

Yellow is the color of the sun and the imperial color of old China. It is the color of gold, of the crystals calcite, citrine, topaz and yellow jade. Yellow heightens your energy and can help make you feel warm and joyous.

Orange is a stimulating color, but being a mixture of red and yellow it does not have the strength of either red or yellow. The positive side of this is that when yellow or red radiate too much energy for you, orange is a gentler alternative. Orange is one of the colors of sunsets and sunrises and of the crystals carnelian, citrine and orange calcite.

Red is one of the most compelling colors for humans, along with black and white. It has formidable energy, so should be used with care. Too much red is never a good thing, for it can be overpowering. If you need a boost in energy, wearing red will help. The closer to the horizon the sun is, the redder it will seem — sometimes a setting sun will appear to set the sea on fire. Red crystals are garnets, carnelian, red jasper and rubies.

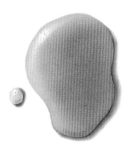

Magenta is a cool red as it contains some blue. Its effect is sensuous and quietly exciting. Magenta is a very strong color, so too much becomes cloying and oppressive. A crystal of this color is rhodalite garnet.

Purple is a combination of red and blue. Depending on the amounts of each hue used, this mixture ranges from the palest of lilacs, mauves and lavenders through to the violets and rich purples. Purple is a color that is associated with the Church and royalty from Europe and ancient Egypt. Great skill is needed to use purple well, otherwise it can be vulgar and unsettling. Amethyst, alexandrite and fluorite are both crystals of purple coloring.

Blue is a color that can be either peaceful and relaxing or cold. It can sometimes bring out feelings of fear and insecurity, depending on its shade and your mood and personality type. The sky and the sea show blue is all its aspects. It is a color that has always carried both positive and negative associations. Blue crystals include blue agate, azurite, lapis lazuli and sapphire.

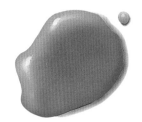

Turquoise is greenish blue and is the color of shallow tropical waters. This is a gentle, peaceful color that will cheer you up. It suits most people and creates a happy, carefree appearance for those who wear it. The legend of the turquoise, a stone in various shades of greenish blue, is that it should always be received as a gift and never purchased. It was often given to a loved one or to someone about to go on a journey. Aquamarine is a crystal of another shade of greenish blue.

Green is everywhere in nature — it is the color of life and is the most restful color to the eye. In its artificial form green can be either peaceful or oppressive, and while some people wear it well, it can make others look sick. Of all the ancient pigments, green ones were the most difficult to obtain. Crystals in shades of green include aventurine, chrysoprase, emerald, jade and malachite.

Primary Colors

Most people regard red, blue and yellow as the primary colors — they are the colors from which all others derive and which cannot be made by mixing together any other colors. These colors are, however, just one set of primary colors — the primary colors for paint — and is the basis of the color wheel below. It shows how, by mixing any two of the three primary colors, you can make secondary colors, and by mixing a secondary color with a primary color you produce a tertiary color. Colors can be mixed or have white or gray added to them to produce as many variations of hue and intensity as you choose.

It is important to realize that there is a difference between mixing paint colors and mixing the colors of light. The primary colors of light are the "additive" colors of red, blue and green, and the "subtractive" colors of magenta (reddish blue), cyan (greenish blue) and yellow. "Additive" means color is added to a surface by colored light beams (transmission of colored light); "subtractive" means the pigments in a surface absorb certain colors from light, reflecting others which when combined give the impression of one color.

Painter's color wheel

Primary Colors of "Additive" and "Subtractive" Color Mixing — Light and Pigment

Additive primary colors — the colors from which all other colors of light are derived — when combined in equal amounts produce white light. Additive primary colors are red, green and blue, and their secondary colors are cyan, yellow and magenta. Practical applications for additive color mixing are used in stage lighting, decorative lighting, and color healing therapies. The principles of additive primary colors are at the basis of color television and color photography.

Subtractive primary colors are the result of pigments absorbing one color and reflecting the others back (see page 8). When subtractive primary colors are combined in equal amounts the color brownish black is produced. Subtractive primary colors are cyan, yellow and magenta, their secondary colors being red, green and blue. All the colors in books and magazines are produced using cyan, yellow, magenta and black inks (color-absorbing pigments), after a process of photographing the images through filters of the additive primary colors (transmission of colored light), and so the greatest intensity of color is achieved.

It is interesting to note that the primaries for one are the secondary colors for the other. See the box to understand how this happens.

Primary Colors of Light

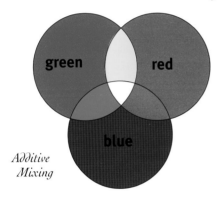

Additive Mixing

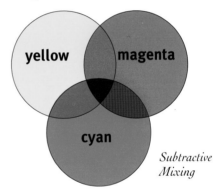

Subtractive Mixing

Additive and Subtractive Primary Colors

Additive: Red light, green light, blue light
Subtractive: Red-absorbing pigment leaves green and blue = cyan
Green-absorbing pigment leaves red and blue = magenta
Blue-absorbing pigment leaves red and green = yellow

Secondary Colors

Additive
Red + green = yellow
Red + blue = magenta
Blue + green = cyan

Subtractive
Cyan + yellow = green
Yellow + magenta = red
Magenta + cyan = blue

Complementary Colors

Complementary colors are contrasting or color opposites, as shown in the color wheel on page 36. The complementary color of a primary color will be the mixture of the other two primary colors. Put near each other in appropriate circumstances, a primary color and its complementary color will give pleasurable contrast. If you mix primary paint color with its complementary, say red and green, both colors will be neutralized. If you beamed light through a green filter on top of a red filter, both the red and the green wavelengths will be neutralized, but yellow light will emerge.

Afterimage

If you stare for at least 30 seconds at a pattern or colored object, then stare at a blank white surface, you will see the image of the pattern or object glowing there in its complementary colors. The same applies if you close your eyes after looking at a colored object. The first image that appears against the darkness is that of the object in its complementary colors.

Try this exercise using the chart below. Stare at the first box for 30 seconds, then look at the white box. Try this exercise with the chart below. Stare at the first box for 30 seconds, then look at the white box.

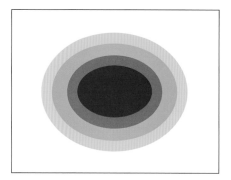 

Warm and Cool Colors

Warm colors are those with yellows or reds in them (greenish yellow to reddish violet range); cool colors are those containing blue (violet to green range). There are, however, warm blues and cool reds. A touch of red or yellow added to blue will warm it; if you add a little blue to red you will cool it. Another factor in the degree of warmth or coolness of a color will depend on its intensity of hue and the colors next to it. While blue is a cool color, if it is pale and surrounded by intense yellow it will appear warm; similarly a pale yellow, surrounded by intense gray blue, will appear cool.

Color Saturation

A pure color is when no white, gray or black is present. When white, gray or black is added, the pigment is modified and lighter or darker colors are produced

Some Aspects of Color

Hue is the color itself, e.g. red, green, blue, purple.

Tone is a color's degree of lightness (high tone) or darkness (low tone). Tonal values are very important to the painter or the photographer for this is what gives form and contrast to the picture. Tones are most clearly seen in a black and white representation of a picture or a black and white photograph.

Chromatic colors are colors of intense hue.

Achromatic colors are colors that have been mixed with white or black, thus lessening the purity of the pigment. Black, white and the grays are also considered achromatic.

Iridescence is the shimmering of colors producing rainbow effects. It can be seen on soap bubbles, a film of oil, fish scales, and the wings of certain insects, among many other animate and inanimate things. Iridescence is caused by interference of light, refraction and diffraction when the position of an object carrying these characteristics is changed.

Color Harmony

If a picture, room or fashion outfit is to be pleasing to all who see it, you must consider some principles of color harmony. Colors are harmonious when a dominant tone and color (see example in the painting below) runs through the others in varying degrees, giving all of them something in common. Balancing color design is another way of achieving harmony. For instance, if you have a patch of green at the left-hand corner of your painting, you could have a small stroke of green near the top right hand corner to achieve balance. Similarly, when decorating a room, try to put small amounts of a dominating color at various points throughout the room — in paintings, ornaments, vases and cushions.

Color that is in disharmony will "fall off" a picture, "lunge" across a room, or "strike out" from a fashion outfit.

Interior Au piano,
Lantoine, Fernand,
1876-1956

Contrast

If a painting or an interior design is to have life, there must be some contrast. Indeed, there are times when artists and interior decorators want excitement and drama in their work rather than harmony, and contrast in color and design is the best way to achieve it. For a successful effect, there must be contrast in form, line, color, shadow and light. Complementary colors that are less often seen, such as reddish violet and greenish yellow may work better than a common pairing, such as red and green. Nature has proved very successful in creating both harmony and contrast — just look at any natural scene and you will see this. You too can be as free and successful as nature in this area, but only if you are true to your inner being.

An excess of contrast, or contrast insensitively applied, will create disharmony and a sense of unease in all who are exposed to it.

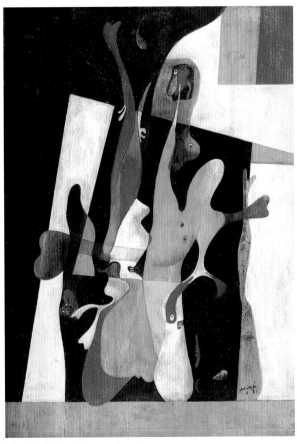

Untitled, *Miró, Joan, 1893-1983*

41

Contour, Tone and Form

People often speak of a woman's "contours". This is what they say when describing her shape. Contours are the outlines that create shapes. Tone is the result of all the variations of light and shade that creates form. Contour does not make use of tone and confines forms within a rigid outline — this, without the use of tone, makes the forms flat. Before the Renaissance, painters outlined all the forms they depicted, thus separating them from their surroundings. At the beginning of the Renaissance, painters began using tone to soften the edges and objects within the pictures, and so the objects merged to some extent with the backgrounds.

Contours are used either to emphasize certain areas of the picture for contrast or for the effect in themselves in modern painting, for flat forms retain the greatest intensity of hue. Strong contrasts of light and shade automatically create contours.

While contours are used to produce flat effects in designs, form is created by softening contours using gentle gradations of tone and hue to produce roundness.

A Still Life of Lemons
and Oranges,
Mensaque, A., FL C. 1863

42

Patterns and Shapes

Patterns and shapes will always create a psychological response from us, depending on what colors are used, how much they contrast with one another, and how severe or free of form they are.

Not everyone will react in the same way at any given time to the same pattern or shape. Generally, however, depending on our mood and personality, we tend to look at squares and feel a sense of security or of being boxed in. Free forms can make you want to fly or flee for cover. Triangles can make you want to reach up if they are pointing upward and dig deeper if they are pointing down. Circles join up and leave no loose ends, so they can generate feelings of security and encourage a contained flow of thought.

Look at each of the illustrations and note how they affect you. Write down your responses. On another day, in another mood, look at them again and write down your responses.

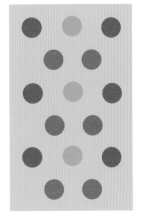

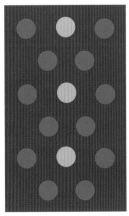

HEALING WITH COLOR

As you have seen so far, color is infinitely more profound than our appreciation of its aesthetic qualities. Light is living energy that is made up of both the visible spectrum (perceived by us as color) and the non-visible spectrum. Light penetrates everything except the deepest seas and the darkest holes deep beneath the earth's surface. Our own bodies are penetrated by light, so we are affected by its properties from our conception — even when we are blind. And many people believe that the light at the center of our etheric selves illuminates outward into the world.

Light makes things grow. An absence of light can cause things to die. It is reasonable therefore to assume that color can heal us, as has been professed from the time of the ancients in Egypt, China, Greece, India and Tibet. Color healing in various forms is still practiced by many people in these cultures and by tribal groups all over the world.

There is a strong interconnection between the vibrations of colors, our own physical vibrations, our emotional vibrations, and vibrations of another sort that may be seen as deriving from personality at its deepest unconscious level, etheric or spiritual. Today there are many techniques of color healing practiced in the West.

Color Therapies

Color therapies or "photobiotics" are alternative healing treatments that use the frequencies of color and light to balance and harmonize the body's organs individually and the person as a whole. For instance, if you have a blood pressure problem, you can use blue light to lower your blood pressure and red light to raise it. The use of complementary (opposite or secondary) pairs of colors (see page 38) are an essential aspect of color therapy. The complementary pairs used in color therapy are red and cyan, orange and blue, yellow and violet, green and magenta Most color therapies are designed to balance both your physical and emotional states and many involve a diagnosis of your aura and your chakras. Your aura is the rainbow of colors that surrounds you and reveals to those who can see it, underactive and overactive emotional and physical conditions. The chakras are the seven major energy centers in our bodies. They radiate certain colors and each color reveals strengths and weaknesses in that area of your life.

Because every person has a different set of vibrations, everyone will respond to a greater or lesser degree to the various colors. The color therapist will find which colors work best for you and adapt his or her techniques to accommodate your particular needs.

A number of color therapies are derived from ancient systems of color healing. Some incorporate the system of color healing associated with the Tree of Life from the Jewish mystical tradition of the kabbala. Others use the mandala, the ancient Buddhist design of a circle enclosing a square, symbolizing the universe, which is used to focus the mind in meditation. The patterns, shapes, symbols and colors of each mandala used will elicit particular responses, so it can be a potent tool in color healing. Many techniques involve the traditional colors associated with the zodiac.

Color therapists may use breathing, meditation, visualization, colored light, candles, paints, crystals, colored fabrics, solarized water, diet of correct "color" foods, essential oils and colored oils made from herbs, flowers and exposure to sunlight. Beaming colored light through filters onto specific parts of the body is one of the most effective of these techniques. The filters are red, orange, yellow, lemon, green, cyan (greenish blue), blue, indigo (dark blue), violet, purple and magenta.

Techniques of color therapy used by psychotherapists who specialize in creative therapies do not employ the same principles as those used by color therapists in the area of health and well-being, though a talented psychotherapist can occasionally effect some remarkable physical healing in the process. Color therapists are concerned with their clients' own color associations emanating from their unconscious minds, thus providing the basis of a successful emotional healing. A part of an exercise a color therapist might use is given on pages 56 and 57.

The Chakras — What Are They?

The chakras represent energy centers and give us a system through which we can understand the constant flow of energy through and around our bodies. The word chakra comes from the Sanskrit for "wheel". The chakras have been studied and written about for centuries in the East, and more recently in the West. As often occurs with knowledge that is very old and drawn from many sources, there is conflicting information on chakras. Most systems, however, recognize that there are many of these energy centers. The seven discussed below are considered the main ones and correspond to the seven most visible colors in the spectrum.

In color healing, the practitioner must first decide which chakra, or chakras, is out of balance and whether it is underactive or overactive. A color therapy technique is then decided upon and applied.

Base chakra

The first chakra is located at the base of the spine. Its corresponding color is red.

This energy center relates to the physical body rather than our emotions and is linked with our survival instinct. It provides courage to stand and fight or the stamina and energy to take flight when our survival is threatened. From the base chakra comes the sexual energy to reproduce and ensure the survival of our species. This chakra also represents our connection with the earth.

Belly chakra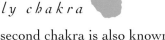

The second chakra is also known as the sacral plexus and is located approximately midway between the base of the spine and the navel. Its corresponding color is orange.

This chakra is the source of our creative energy and our desires and passions. It is associated with our emotions, intuition and sexuality and is connected to the element of water.

Solar plexus chakra

The third chakra is located just above the navel and is the chakra that relates to how we interact with the world around us. Its corresponding color is yellow.

From this center comes our personal power and our energy to act. The solar plexus is the point of intersection between the physical and the mental.

Heart chakra

The fourth chakra is located in the center of the body at the level of the heart. Its corresponding color is green.

This chakra inspires our love: romantic and sexual love, as well as love for the world and everything in it. It gives us compassion and understanding, and helps us develop our sense of relationship with others and our place in the world. From the heart chakra we can understand how all things relate to each other and to ourselves.

Throat chakra

The fifth chakra is located at the throat. Its corresponding color is blue.

This is the chakra of communication, of how we express ourselves in the world, both verbally and non-verbally and how we receive information from the world. The throat chakra is involved with the silent communications that take place within our bodies through the workings of the nervous system and the endocrine system.

Brow chakra

The sixth chakra is located at the center of the forehead. This chakra is also known as the third-eye chakra. Its corresponding color is indigo.

Through our third eye we receive information through our perceptions and gain insight and a deeper level of understanding. Developing the energy at this chakra involves an increased level of awareness, enabling us to access our inner wisdom.

Crown chakra

The seventh chakra is located at the top of the head. Its corresponding color is violet or purple.

The crown chakra is the source of our thoughts, our conscious and unconscious minds, our beliefs and dreams. It connects to our inner sense of "knowing" and is the intersecting point between our mind and our body.

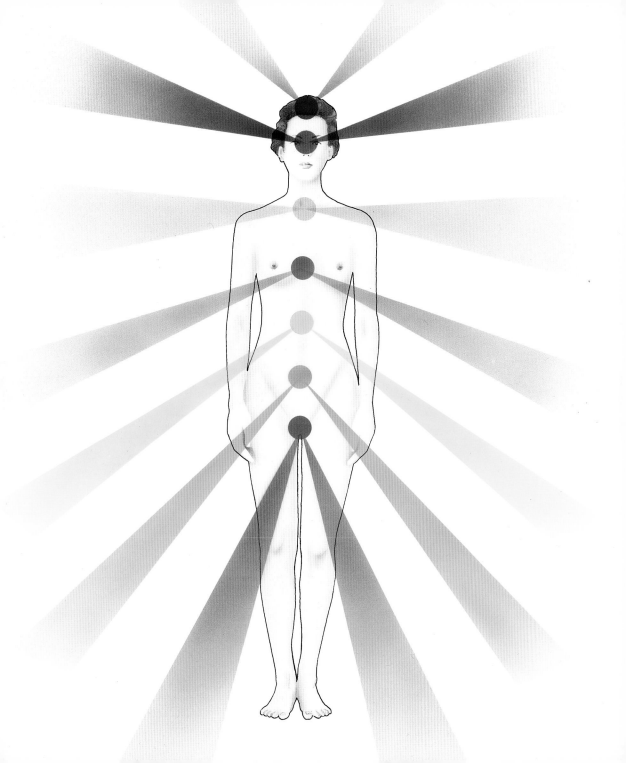

What is Your Aura?

A human aura is an egg-shaped kaleidoscopic play of color which extends around your body to a distance of up to three feet (1 meter). There are several layers to your aura, the closest one to your body being your etheric body. Your energy centers are within this layer and their purpose is to draw and absorb the life-force from the atmosphere.

When an aura is healthy, its colors are pure, luminous and in perfect harmony. When you have a physical or emotional problem, certain colors will be muddy, depending on what your problems are. The more ill or disturbed you are, the dirtier and darker the colors will be. The shape and pattern of your aura will also be affected.

Your aura reflects your physical, emotional and spiritual conflicts. A healer who can see your aura will know at once the basis of your problem, and can then take steps to help you heal, but he or she can only do this with your assistance. No healing is a *fait accompli*. It is not uncommon for a healer to see discords in your aura long before any illness manifests. This is because weaknesses are present in your body before an illness takes hold, and these make their appearance in your aura. Steps can then be taken to prevent the illness from developing further.

The Meanings of the Colors of the Perfect Aura

Gold is only present where there is great intellect as well as high spiritual development.

White represents purity and high spiritual evolvement.

Red relates to the physical body and sexuality. It shows a vibrant personality, someone who sets the spirit on fire.

Orange is the energy of the life-force. It shows joy and lightheartedness.

Yellow represents the astral body and corresponds to the third chakra.

Greens and **blues** show the state of your health. Green also represents the personality.

Violets and **purples** are psychically evolved colors. They represent the higher self and the spirit.

Any variation or imbalance in these colors will show dysfunction. Grays and murky colors especially indicate ill-health and depression.

Crystals, Color and Healing

There is some evidence to suggest that crystals resonate with the frequency of healthy cells, drawing unhealthy cells that may be vibrating at a lower or higher frequency back into the normal range by a process called "entrainment".

Since every cell in our body has its own frequency, this may explain why some crystals work most effectively on a particular part of the body and why different crystals benefit different people.

When deciding which stones to use for healing and where they should be placed on the body, trust your intuition. If you instinctively feel you would like to use a particular stone or feel drawn to it when thinking about a particular part of the body, use the crystal and judge the results for yourself. If you don't have a piece of a crystal specified in the chakra layout below, use one of a similar color. The color of the crystal should relate to the color emitted by the specific chakras.

Cleansing Your Crystals

Make sure all the crystals you are about to use have been cleansed. Some crystals transform energies and others absorb or transmit them, so inappropriate or undesirable patterns of energy need to be cleared away. By doing this you also attune the crystal's energies to your own.

There are many methods you can use, such as moonbaths (placing crystals in a glass or ceramic bowl filled with cold water and set under the light of a full moon overnight); sunbaths (follow same directions but placing the bowl under the noon sun for one to two hours); returning them to the earth (burying the crystals in a potted plant or in rich soil for two to three days); or moving the crystal through the smoke of burning sage. The simplest method is to meditate and imagine any negativity falling away from the crystal, leaving it clear, clean and vibrant.

Using Crystals to Heal

Lie on your back and put the crystals into position as described below, starting at the crown chakra. Stay in this position, breathing deeply and slowly for about 15 minutes. Slowly remove the crystals, starting at the crown and working downward.

Crown chakra: Place a single clear quartz crystal a short distance away from the top of the head. If using a terminated crystal, angle the point toward the head — this directs the crystal's energy into the crown chakra.

Brow chakra: Place a single point of amethyst, a piece of tumbled amethyst or purple fluorite over the brow chakra.

Throat chakra: For the throat chakra use a piece of aquamarine or jade on the throat, over the voice box.

Heart chakra: Place a small piece of uncut or tumbled rose quartz crystal over the heart chakra.

Solar plexus: Place a single point, a small cluster or a tumbled piece of citrine over the solar plexus. If using a terminated crystal, position so the point of the stone is facing toward the head or facing upward, away from the body.

Belly chakra: Place a piece of carnelian or red jasper halfway between the solar plexus and the base of the spine.

Base chakra: Place a single point or tumbled stone of smoky quartz over the base of the spine. If using a terminated crystal, position so the point of the stone is facing toward to the head.

Color in Psychology

Color symbolism can be a very individual thing. Green, for instance, might symbolize life for some and decay for others. Red can be an energizer and a positive color of power for some, or a color of overwhelming heat and oppression for others. Each color has its own wavelength and each of us emit energies that vary from those of other people, at different times and for different emotions. It is only natural, therefore, that our responses to various colors will differ from those of other people — sometimes a little, at other times a lot. These individual differences are taken into account during color therapy.

Identifying Your Colors

One way to discover your personal colors is to look at a range of colors from their most pure form through their various shades. Glance quickly at each one on the page opposite and take note of that first impression — do not try to analyze it. You will find that some colors make you feel good while others bring up negative reactions. Certain colors will do nothing for you at all, so dismiss them and concentrate on the ones that evoke the strongest reactions from you.

Look at each one separately and try to merge your consciousness with it for as long as it takes to allow yourself to be fully absorbed into the experience of the color. Does this color have a temperature? Are you experiencing tactile sensations, such as rough, smooth, hard, soft, or do you feel as though you can float through it? Does this color take you back to a time in your past? Does it bring up images or a specific memory, no matter how fractured? Is there a sense of smell attached to it? Taste? Sound? And what emotions are you experiencing from this color?

Take notes of your experiences of the colors you have chosen and you will know what each of these colors can do for you to enrich your experience of life.

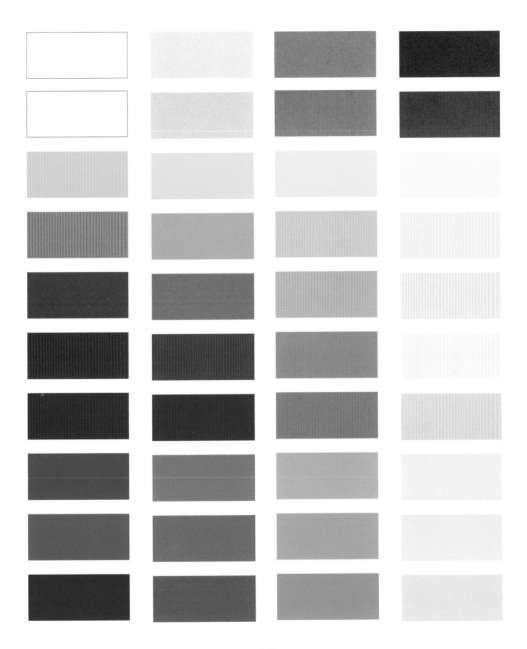

A Color Visualization

There are many techniques of color visualization. They are all designed to help soothe and balance your emotions, and there are some that can isolate negative feelings and help heal them.

If you were to do color therapy with a creative therapist, he or she may give you an exercise like the one described below as a first step in clarifying your underlying feelings. It involves a combination of visualization and using paints, colored pencils or crayons to concretize your emotions. This way, you can identify what's bothering you, look at it, draw it, then objectify it. The next step involves "letting go" of this feeling, though you may need a therapist to help you do this.

When something is bothering you or you are not feeling quite right, tune into whatever emotions you are experiencing. For example: Do you feel tense, fearful, vacant, depressed, angry? Don't know? It doesn't matter. Close your eyes. Allow yourself to freely experience this feeling without judgment. Now separate yourself from the feeling and observe it.

Talk about it, either to the person with you or, if you are alone, into a tape recorder. Describe what the feeling looks like — its shape, its size, its color. Can you touch it? If so, how does it feel — hard, soft, rough, smooth, wet or dry?

When you have elicited as much information as you can, take your paints or pencils and draw your image on a large sheet of paper. When you look at what you've painted or drawn you will see, objectively, a range of aspects of this emotion in your own symbolism. Notice how you feel about the emotion now.

All this exercise takes is your willingness to allow yourself free access to your psyche. The more you go into and then out of your psyche, the freer you will be — creatively and psychically, and your perceptions of yourself and the world will become more vivid.

I recently felt a surge of anger, so I took the opportunity to visualize this feeling and then paint it (see opposite). A creative therapist would ask me to become the red and describe how I feel, using all the questions outlined above; she would ask me to go into every part of the red — the dense color, the shapes, the watery effects on its edge; she would ask me to become the black; and she would ask me to become the red key-like symbol in the black.

As we know, red can represent anger and it can represent power. Carl Jung among others theorized that we have one pool of energy that we can utilize how we choose, in love, hate, power, anger, joy or depression.

In taking me through my painting, the creative therapist's purpose would be to help me harness the energy of anger and transform it into positively directed, empowering energy.

Using Color to Alter Your Mood

Most people have favorite colors. These colors usually make them feel good, which in turn makes others feel good to be around them. However, your favorite color is not always the color that will make you feel on top of the world.

People who are sensitive to color will be aware that on some days even their favorite color will not improve their mood, so they choose something else that will give them vitality, if that's what they lack, or calm, if they are feeling anxious or angry. While many people decide the night before what they are going to wear to work, some people will not do this because they don't know what mood they will wake up with. They often have their closets arranged by color so that they can go directly to the color they know will improve their sense of well-being.

For instance, if red is your favorite color, it would not be a good idea to wear it when you are feeling anxious or angry, for it will only encourage you to overreact to small incidents or to lash out at someone, actions that you will sooner or later regret. The best colors for you to wear in such a mood, depending on what colors suit you and your personal likes and dislikes, would be creams, greens, grays and blues, for they will calm you and help neutralize the intensity of your explosive mood. Likewise, if you are feeling depleted of energy or just plain down, then red is a positive color to wear, for it increases your energy and awakens your spirits.

Patterns will also affect your mood. Patterns that create a sense of fast movement or jagged rhythms will intensify anxiety or irritation. Paisley patterns or flower patterns in subtle colors or patterns with gently flowing shapes will lower your emotional temperature.

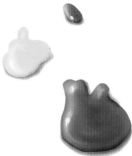

Zoe Abbott, age 12.

Color in the Home

The basic colors of the walls, the ceilings and the floor coverings of the place where you live are important when it comes to your moods. We should feel relaxed and contented when we're at home; but often, especially in rental accommodation, we walk through the door and experience some negative emotion. And we generally don't know why this is.

You might realize that you don't like the color scheme of your house, but you might not be aware that the colors may actually be toxic to you. Even if you are renting a place, there are things you can do without a great deal of expense to neutralize such negative effects. Look at pages 54 and 55 to see what colors are beneficial to you and for what reasons.

When deciding on your color scheme, it is important to take into account the size of the room, how much light it gets, your own personal likes and dislikes, whether you prefer warm or cool colors, and in what situation you favor these colors. Everyone is different. And remember that highly colored paintings and other decorations can warm up cool colors and give relief to large expanses of neutral colors.

Rugs from the cheapest Indian dhurrie to the most fabulous Persian rug will enhance a wooden floor or lift neutral colored carpet. If you are in a rental, you can't expect the landlord to buy you new carpet, but you can buy an inexpensive creamy colored Indian cotton or wool rug that will hide most of the dirty green, brown or orange that you currently live with.

Brighten up drab furniture with vivid cushions and colorful nick-nacks and ornaments. This is one area where you can afford to let yourself go with color. Chairs do not have to match — a variety of colors and styles will create an individual atmosphere.

Color at Work

Until recently, industry, hospitals and schools paid no attention to color. They opted for uncontroversial hues such as indeterminate grays, creams and greens, colors that were oppressive and depressing to most of the people who were exposed to them. Patients in hospitals probably felt sicker and less optimistic about recovery; teachers in schools tended to transmit information to their students in the form of basic facts without using their imaginations; and the drab colors of industry imbued those in control with a no-nonsense attitude and the workers with low morale.

Nowadays there is a greater consciousness of the psychological effects of color. Management in hospitals, industry and other places of business employ specialists to design color schemes that will bring out the best in both employees and clients.

In hospitals this new awareness can be seen most clearly in children's wards. Colorful images of cartoon characters decorate the walls; brightly colored bedspreads, games and toys abound. The doctors and nursing staff are more cheerful and children feel a little better about being sick.

Industry now uses colors to increase worker morale and productivity. For instance, bright colors in the factory will lessen the boredom created by repetitive tasks. Warm, neutral colors are useful in classrooms where students need to feel relaxed yet energized.

Your Personal Work Area

While you are unlikely to be able to make major changes in your work area, such as painting the walls or removing the carpet, you can decorate your personal space or office with colorful objects that have meaning for you. Vases and flowers, crystals, paintings, photographs and colorful containers for your work tools are just some of the things you can use to lift your working environment.

Enhance Your Personal Appeal With Color

Colored fabrics act as filters of light and they can either enhance your sense of well-being or conflict with your energies, thus causing a feeling of disturbance. Using the exercise and its corresponding color chart on pages 54 and 55, determine which colors have the most profound effect on you. Discover which colors make you feel energized; which ones induce a state of relaxation and sense of calm; and those that make you feel sensuous.

People respond to you according to how you project yourself to them. To project the image you most desire, it is important that the colors you wear bring out desirable aspects of your personality. If you are trying to attract a new lover, for instance, you should not wear a color that is supposed to be sexy unless it feels sexy to you.

Your attractiveness to a potential partner comes from your vibrations rather than your actual appearance. The color red is known to be a color that stimulates passion, sex and love. It is the color of the base chakra which is responsible for energizing your sexual drive. However, if red makes you feel over-stimulated, or you just don't feel right about wearing red, then it is not going to create a positive effect on a possible lover. Magenta may be a color that makes you feel warm and sensuous, so this would be a color you could use in your personal space or in your clothing. The nature of the fabric also contributes to the effect of the color. Magenta silk will have a more intimate and delicate effect than a magenta-colored wool, linen or cotton.

How Much Color Can a Lover Take?

Common wisdom says that red and the warm colors are the most sensuous. But any color can be sensuous if you wear it well and it enhances the positive aspects of your own vibrations. Strong color must be used with caution, because too much of any potent color could have an overwhelming effect on both you and your partner, rather like the effect of eating too much rich dessert. It is also important to realize that emitting a vibration of eroticism is only a small aspect of being sexy.

Mystery is sexy, yet red, orange and magenta are hardly mysterious — grays, silvers and blacks can be, if you know how to present them and accessorize them. Fun is sexy, and red, yellow and orange, as well as aqua and turquoise, are associated with playfulness. Some people find the combination of beauty and distance sensuous — the ivories, grays, gray-blues and silvers fall into this category. However, the fabrics should be silks, satins, velvets and cashmere — gray cotton is seldom sensuous — and a flash of one of the erotic colors in the form of a jewel, silk scarf or velvet cushion on the settee could set a potential partner on fire. But for those lovers who desire an overtly open, playful partner will prefer gentle shades of red, yellow and orange.

Erotic colors are usually the strong, stimulating colors, such as intense reds, yellows and oranges. Too much of any of these colors, however, or if they are used in the wrong way or on the wrong fabric, will over-stimulate and actually repel a potential lover, so use them with caution. If red is too strong for you, try some clear orange or yellow, perhaps together, in fine fabrics.

The age-old sentiment of hold back
and don't give everything at once
also applies to the use of color.

How the Wrong Use of Color Can Affect You

As we have seen, light comes from the sun through the atmosphere. It reacts with pigments in all things, including humans. In addition, people emit their own inner light. Because everyone has a different set of pigments in their skin, hair and eyes, and everyone emits a different set of energy patterns, a "wrong" color will not be the same for everyone.

Dull Colors

What are dull colors? Beige, gray, brown, grayish hues of bright colors? It depends the purity of each of these colors, on who is wearing them, with what, and in which context. For instance, people with rich dark brown hair, a fresh complexion and a fit physique will look marvelous in beige, as indeed they will in any color they choose. Beige will give a soft contrast to their dramatic appearance, and contrast is always good.

Beige will be dull when worn by someone with mousy hair and a pale complexion, regardless of his or her physique. This person will give off a beige vibration and other people will barely notice him or her. However, if this person were to accessorize with gold yellows, clear warm greens, scarlets or even a rich black, the beige would suddenly come alive.

The problem comes when a person wants to disappear into the background and dresses in beiges and grays so that he or she won't be noticed by the rest of the world. People who feel this way are allowing their insecurities to rule their lives. If you feel this way, ask yourself how, in an ideal world, you would wish to be seen. When you find the answer, pretend you are this person, read the exercise on page 54 and look at the color chart on page 55, then become that person.

Bright Colors

Bright colors are wonderful and almost everybody loves them, but they should be used in small doses. Some people who love bright colors wear too much of them and their own personalities become hidden behind the frenetic vibrations the colors create. Most people will shy away from so much intensity. Bright colors will also intensify any feelings of anxiety or anger.

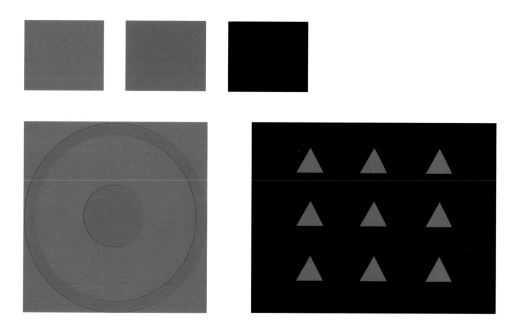

Powerful colors need to be broken up, either by those that are less vivid or by a combination of darker or lighter contrasting colors. For instance, a flat, scarlet red silk jacket makes a very bold statement. While this works for some people, it may create an impression that is stronger than you would like. That same jacket embroidered with a delicate flower design in dark cool green, some turquoise, soft violets, whites and even pinks becomes a piece that combines drama with delicacy, boldness with subtlety. The Chinese, Japanese and Indians are masters of this art of color and mood balance.

The Clash of Color

In nature nothing clashes. This may be because the colors that constitute the broadest spaces — green foliage, blue skies and seas, beige sands and fields, earth red and ochre deserts — are easy on the eye. The vivid colors in nature appear in small amounts, in flowers, in birds, and in tiny insects.

A clash occurs when two colors of equal intensity and quantity are put together, for instance, red and green or yellow and hot pink. However, a large amount of red that has the right shade(s) of green delicately scattered over it can be very pleasing; and a yellow shirt would look good when worn with a scarf that has a delicate design including touches of hot pink.

The truth is that the clash of color is a subjective notion. It would be a good idea, though, when deciding on your outfit for the day, that you "feel" the colors and become aware of how they are affecting you. If the feelings are right then wear them, otherwise choose something else.

THE CREATIVE WORLD OF COLOR

The creative world of color is open for everyone to enjoy and experiment with to create beauty of their own. This chapter shows you some of the ways modern painters approached color. It also lets you know how you can use color creatively to awaken your imagination and expand your sense of being.

An Explosion of Color — The Beginning of Modern Art

The Impressionists

This movement appeared toward the end of the nineteenth century in France and included artists such as Renoir, Monet, Pissaro, Degas and Cezanne, though Cezanne, along with Gauguin and Seurat, departed from the principles of Impressionism early in his career.

The Impressionists were concerned with capturing the effects of light. They banished black and earth colors from their palettes and used the pure colors of the visible spectrum and the effects of light itself to create many other hues. They did not mix colors. Instead, they put dabs or strokes of pure color alongside each other leaving small areas of unpainted white canvas between them. Each dab of color would vibrate across the white spaces, creating other colors — for instance, a dab of pure red and a dab of pure yellow would create an orange light on the intervening white canvas. When you look at these paintings from a distance you get the impression of a whole range of colors, many of which are the combinations of color vibrations.

Vincent Van Gogh

This Dutch artist, whose extraordinary life has been dramatized for films and books, came out of Impressionism. He used bright colors in divided brushstrokes that were more like bars than dabs, and he made no attempt to create any mixing of color vibrations like the Impressionists. Van Gogh's intensity of color was far greater than anything produced before. He developed a color scheme whereby he used two related colors, such as red and orange, together with the complementary of one of them, either green or blue. Van Gogh is one of the most loved painters of all time.

Paysage de Bretagne, *Paul Gauguin, 1848-1903*

The Fauves

Vincent Van Gogh had a profound influence on the Fauves. At the beginning of the Fauve movement, in his figures, landscape and still life, Matisse painted areas in flat pure color rather than using tones to mold them. Other artists from this movement and influenced by Van Gogh painted with explosions of color.

Then the Fauves took the greatest liberty with color. They no longer cared what colors occurred in real life. They painted violet trees and green houses. They also painted different colors on the same tree or house to create contrast and effect.

Joan Miró

Influenced by the Expressionists and the Fauves, Miró was one of the first Surrealists, those painters who transformed reality into symbolism. He used broad expanses of color, often very bright color, in various shapes and designs. He frequently used black panels and flowing black lines and strange figures and shapes, which made the colors even brighter.

The Power of Color and Your Creativity

"I wish I were creative" is something that many people say. The fact is that everyone is born creative. Getting in touch with your creativity involves realizing which creative area you find most exciting, then freeing your psyche from your intellect and letting it all come out, without making negative judgments about what you produce. Remember, colors are an expression of your unconscious mind — you don't have to understand their significance, you need only feel them.

Finding Your Own Creative Area

Everyone has an affinity with some creative area or another. Often, people don't realize that something they are drawn to is actually creative. Anything that excites passion in you is a means through which you can express your creativity, no matter how banal it might appear to others. So, the first step is to find out what brings out that feeling of excitement in you. While many people love music and wish they could play an instrument, they are not prepared to put in all the hours per day and the years of practice required to perform like a concert artist. However, anyone who loves music can learn to play an instrument to his or her own satisfaction. The same principle applies to all the arts.

Color provides the most accessible and satisfying ways to bring out your creativity. Put a child in front of a pile of colored fabrics and see what he or she does with it. Give the child a palette of bright colors and some paper and watch him or her set to work. You can do the same, except that while the child is uninhibited about the process, you are probably inhibited by your inner critic who is watching over you with an eagle eye.

Michelle McKenzie,
age 5

Dealing with Your Inner Critic

In a nutshell, you must lose your inner critic. Send it away or tell it to go to sleep until you call for it — your inner critic works for you, you do not work for it. Your inner critic will try to prevent you from doing anything that is outside the boundaries of your normal life. Your inner critic is the result of your training to be a responsible human being in society. Very young children have not yet developed their inner critics, despite the attempts made by parents and caregivers to help them do so, so they have no problem with using colors however they choose, or making whatever lines they like or putting color wherever they want. The word "inappropriate" is meaningless to a small child. However, as a child grows, the concepts of appropriateness and of being a good citizen take on more and more weight.

As an adult, in order to regain that creativity you once had, you need to learn to see through child's eyes again, which in turn will help you feel those old excitements and view the world in a fresh and vibrant way.

> *You need to get to a place within yourself where it's okay to do anything you like — without judgment.*

Other Ways to Use Color Creatively

There are many ways to use color to make you feel happy and fulfilled. Some people take great pleasure in decorating their homes or in building up collections of colorful ornaments or certain types of pottery. All these endeavors are creative. However, the material on the following pages is devoted to painting, crafts and gardening.

Painting

The best way to experience the world is through our senses. Children are born in tune with their senses — sight, touch, hearing, smell and taste. As we grow, the intellect gradually assumes importance and we pay less attention to the messages we gather from our senses. What we think we should be doing negates what we would spontaneously and naturally experience.

One excellent way to override the inhibiting aspects of our "socialization" is to indulge in a bit of finger painting. This way we get to touch the paint and experience its texture and smell. When you put your fingers in paint, somehow the colors seem more vivid. This is because you are touching the paint, instead of putting a brush between your clean fingers and its messiness. Finger painting is a potent tactile experience, allowing our unconscious to project itself through our senses to the outside world in the form of a painting. Our unconscious is then reflected back for us to see.

To begin — and don't be surprised if you feel nervous or embarrassed — you can experiment by stroking color onto a piece of paper or old canvas. Try mixing colors and see what happens. You will find that if you mix two colors together you will create other colors, some commonplace, others only you could have created. If you mix more than two colors together other than white (which you use if you want to lighten a color), before applying to the surface, you will get mud. Mixing color on the surface could create some interesting effects. If you are using water-based paints (acrylic, water color, poster color, any children's paints) see what happens if you wet the paper or board first, then gently smear the color into the wetness.

You can paint with your fingertips, your fingernails, the sides of your fingers or the flats of your fingers. You can put your fingers into the pots or tubes of paints to make blobs, thick smears and swirls, or half mix two colors so you have a rainbow effect and apply that. The more inventive you are the more you will enjoy it. Imagine yourself as a pig in a pen, rolling around in the mud in the sun.

When you are ready to paint your picture, have your colors on a palette or a plate, or pure in their tubes if your prefer, then take a piece of board, paper or canvas. Close your eyes and breathe slowly

for a few minutes. When you have reached a state of complete relaxation, let your thoughts float freely — don't try to keep tabs on them.

Stick your fingers into whichever color takes your immediate attention and apply it to your painting surface. Let your finger do whatever it wants to in order to make color on the page. You may like to stroke the color on sometimes, wriggle it on at others, circle it, interact with other colors. Do whatever feels right at the time. The only rule is, don't let your inner critic or your intellect contaminate the experience.

Everything you paint in this way will be individual. I will never be able to reproduce the painting above, because if I go through the same process, another painting will emerge. If I try to copy it, the new picture will have no vitality.

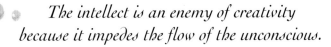 *The intellect is an enemy of creativity because it impedes the flow of the unconscious.*

Crafts — Creating Color From Bits and Pieces

Crafts are a marvelous way to use color creatively. There are so many crafts that you can indulge in, including toys, knitting, rug-making, furnishings, dressmaking, patchwork, spinning and weaving, fabric dying, tapestries and wall-hangings. Here we will look at three of the crafts that can be made from odds and ends that you can pick up from around the house, or materials from old clothing, or the sample bags you can obtain from clothing manufacturers.

Children's Toys

Children's toys are fun to make and because children are not judgmental about color you can make red faces or blue and yellow ones. You can put the "wrong" colors together as often as you like and the kids will love it.

Use scraps of fabrics to make the faces and bodies, strands of wool for hair, and pieces of felt for hands and feet. For eyes and noses, use felt or buttons — but make sure they are very firmly sewn on. You can crochet or knit woolen toys in the weird combinations of colors you have secretly always wanted to use.

Tabletops

You can make spectacular tabletops for the garden or the house by collecting all your broken tiles, dishes, glassware and mirrors. You can decorate an old table already lying around, or obtain one from a junk shop. You will need to decide whether you want to use this table indoors or outside in the garden — mirror pieces create wonderful effects as they reflect the sky, trees and flowers around it. If you wish to use the table outside, then contact a hardware store to find out what materials will weatherproof that table, including the correct glues and fillers required for fixing the pieces onto the table. If it is a wooden table, painting it with a good quality outdoor paint should be sufficient weatherproofing. Before gluing the pieces down, arrange them over the tabletop until you have a design that pleases you.

Another way to decorate old pieces of furniture is to paint designs on them. It is a good idea to do sketches of your design before you start painting, because it can be very difficult to remove paint once it is down.

Patchwork

Patchwork is a wonderful way of recycling fabric remnants. The traditional, formal method requires precision and skill, and if you intend to make a quilt this is probably the best approach. If you want to create decorative throwovers, you can put together fabrics of any color or design next to any other randomly selected piece. This method is a lot of fun and a process of discovery. You will be amazed at how any combination you put together will actually work. The only difficulty that can arise is in fitting together disparate shapes and sizes. Try and cut the fabrics so they fit comfortably with the shapes around them. When you have finished the patchwork, back it with some calico or gingham. Quilts can also be made using this informal method, but precision will still be required if the quilt is to be effective.

Creative Gardening

Gardening is one of the most beautiful things you can do for yourself. When you put your hands into the soil, which is at the essence of life, you are in contact with living color and the energies that emanate from plants and trees and that will regenerate your own. If you only have a balcony or tiny backyard, you can fill that with color in pots and tubs and hanging baskets. Even a window sill can carry a colorful tiny garden in a window box.

There are many landscape design theories about color coordination and grouping in color, but the reality is that no color clashes in nature. While pink and yellow may not be such a great color combination for many people in a fashion outfit, a yellow flower among pink ones lifts the pink and brings an added joy into that area of the garden. Of course there are colors that you don't personally like and there's no need to plant flowers of those hues. Add rocks, stones and even small statues to your garden, as well as bird feeders, hanging baskets, and any other device that will make this a special place for you.

When choosing plants for your garden you need to consider your climatic conditions, your soil types and how much sun your chosen plants require. And do you want perennials — plants that live from year to year — and/or annuals — usually the brightest garden flowers, but they die at the end of each season and need to be replanted. Annuals do, however, provide you with the opportunity to create constant change in your garden.

You can create garden beds of flowing design — curved borders, kidney shapes, whatever your imagination can dream up — or they can be straight rows along pathways and the edges of your lawns. Visualize each of these and note the effect they have on you.

Finding the Best Plants for Your Garden
Go to all your local garden centers as most of them tend to specialize in particular plants as well as having most of the usual plants suitable for your area. If you do not know what soil type you have, take a sample in a plastic bag for an expert to see and test.

When you first arrive, walk around the garden center and see what is available. The tags attached to the plants will inform you of the best conditions for them. Ask one of the employees to walk around with you and tell him or her the colors you would like in your garden, how tall you want your plants to be (a variety is best, the tallest at the back, the shortest at the front), and how much sun the various areas of your garden receives.

Major Plant Groups

Annuals and perennials
Bulbs, corms and tubers
Cacti and succulents
Climbers and creepers
Ferns, palms and cycads
Fruit and nut trees

Ground covers
Orchids
Shrubs
Vegetables and herbs
Indoor plants

INDEX

PICTURE CREDITS

Published by Lansdowne Publishing Pty Ltd
Sydney NSW 2000, Australia

Publisher: Deborah Nixon
Production Manager: Sally Stokes
Project Co-ordinator: Jenny Coren
Designer: Sylvie Abecassis
Illustrations: David Wood
Cover illustration: Sue Ninham

National Library of Australian Cataloguing-in-Publication Data

Blanche, Cynthia, 1952–
The power of color: harness the creative and healing energy of color.

ISBN 1 86302 627 4

1. Color - Therapeutic use. 2. Color - Psychological aspects. I. Title

152.145

Set in Cochin on QuarkXPress
Printed in Singapore by Tien Wah Press (Pte) Ltd
Flag images courtesy of Flag Society of Australia Inc.